FROM THE
BOOK COLLECTION OF:

· · · · · · · · ·

'Give me a museum and I'll fill it.'

Pablo Picasso

to the museums →

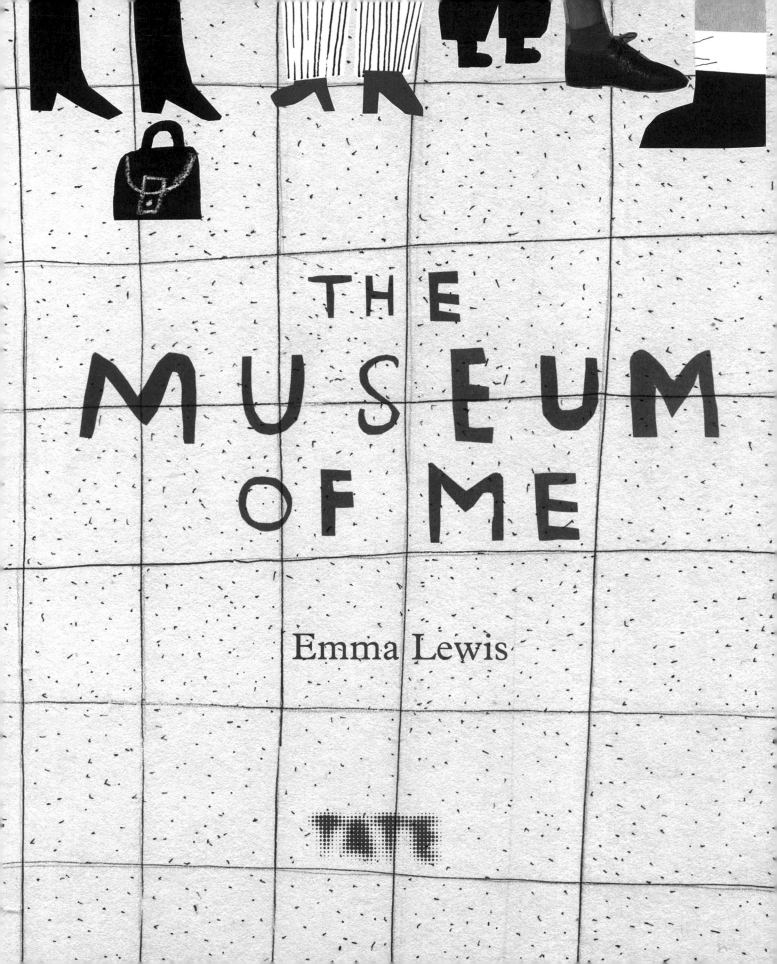

THE MUSEUM OF ME

Emma Lewis

TATE

Everyone says
I'm going to love
the museums.

Museums are big buildings filled with the oldest and oddest things from all around the world.

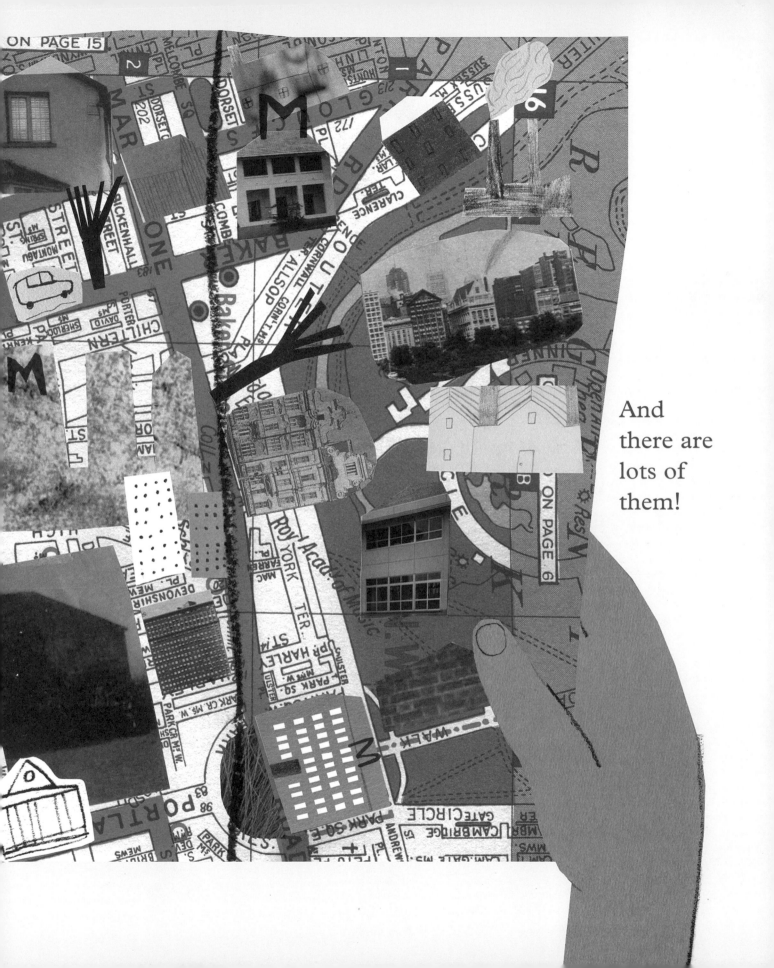

ON PAGE 15

ON PAGE 6

And
there are
lots of
them!

This place
is enormous!

It's the
Museum of
Ancient
Artefacts.

The things inside are *thousands* of years old and from *thousands* of miles away

.and they all
ended up here!

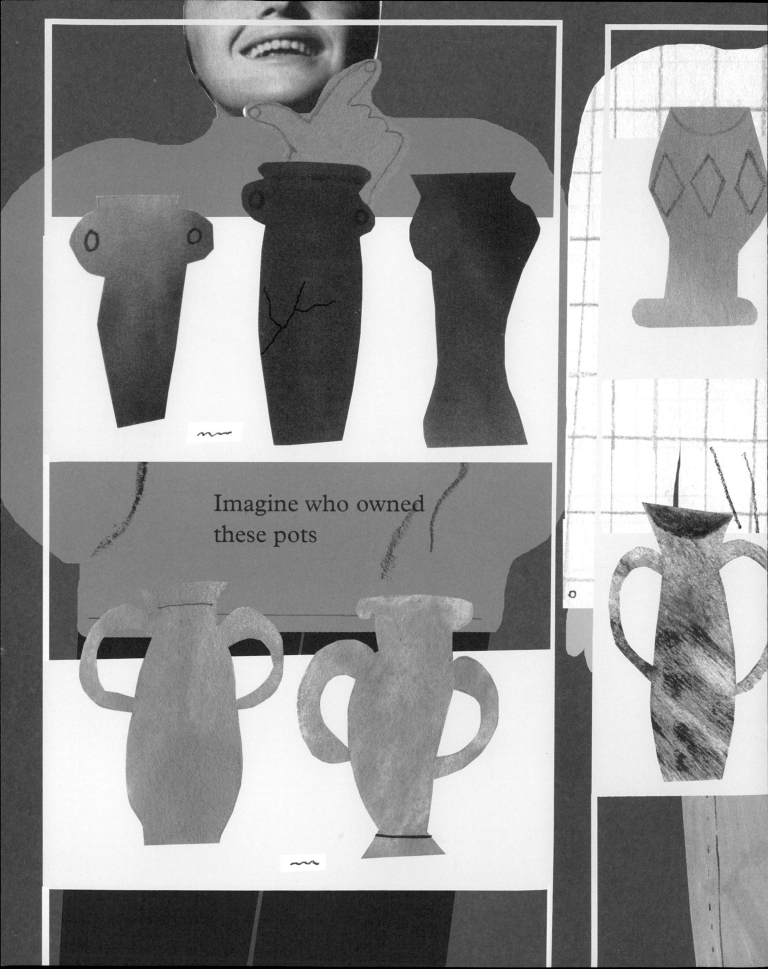

Imagine who owned
these pots

In the Museum
of Natural History
there are giant bugs
and peculiar beasts.

Rooms of
strange birds
I've never
seen before…

BiRDS

HORNBILLS AND TOUCANS

86

And treasures
found deep
underground and
far out at sea,
brought back by
fearless
explorers!

But this
is a collection
that's not
ancient or wild.

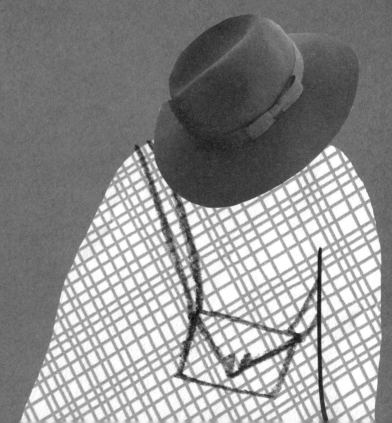

The Museum
of Art is
neither of
those!

Everybody here likes something different.

And you know,
not all museums
are in big
buildings…

NEWS

9 7 0260 9591

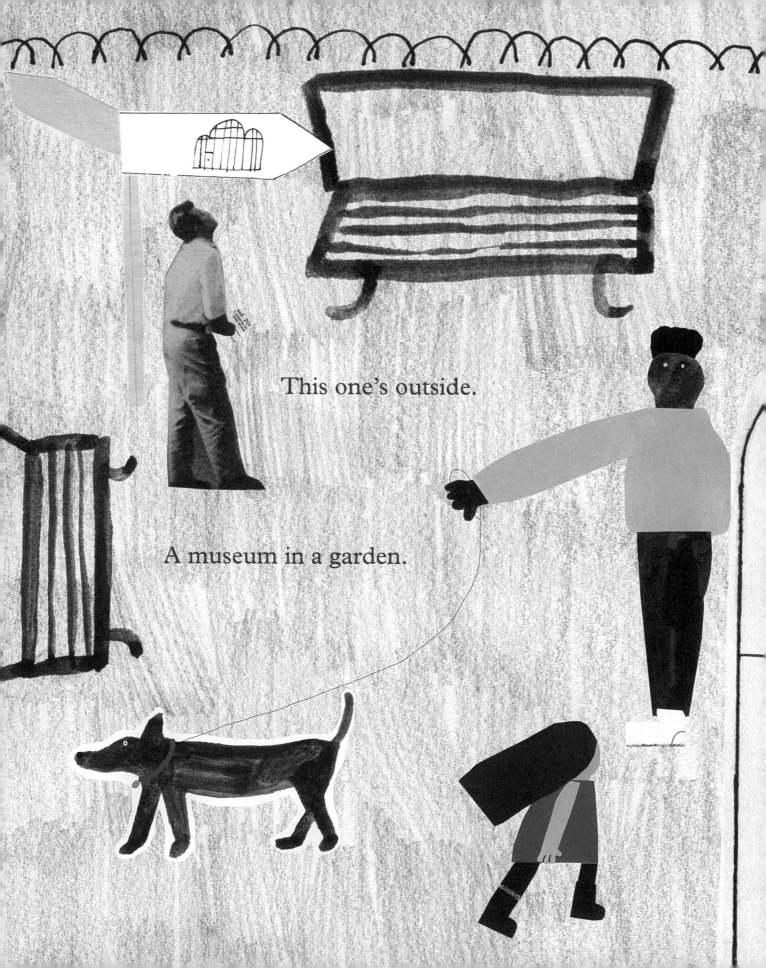

This one's outside.

A museum in a garden.

There are spikey palms
and feathery leaves
and flower heads as big as my own!

A growing collection.

Museums don't have to be old at all!

The Space Museum has all sorts of *new* things.

What kinds of museums do they have up there?

An endless number, an infinity to visit!

But guess which collection
is still left to see?

One that's
full of my
favourite things.

The museum
I know best.

The Museum of Me!

For Mum and Dad

Special thanks to Anna, Alice, Angela and Lizzie

First published 2016 by order of the Tate Trustees
by Tate Publishing, a division of Tate Enterprises Ltd,
Millbank, London SW1P 4RG
www.tate.org.uk/publishing

This paperback edition first published in 2020

© Tate Enterprises Ltd 2016

A catalogue record for this book is available from the British Library

ISBN 978-1-84976-731-6

Distributed in the United States and Canada by ABRAMS, New York
Library of Congress Control Number applied for

Designed by Lizzie Ballantyne

Colour reproduction by Evergreen Colour Management Ltd

Printed in China by Toppan Leefung Printing Ltd

MIX
Paper from
responsible sources
FSC® C104723
FSC
www.fsc.org